Carolyn Wright

Ready, Set, Grow!

American English

Workbook **1**

CAMBRIDGE

Our Book

Hello

Listen. Say. Circle.

Make. **Say.**

①

②

③

④

1 Our Rainbow

 Listen. Color. Say.

Circle. Color. Say.

Listen. Point. Trace.

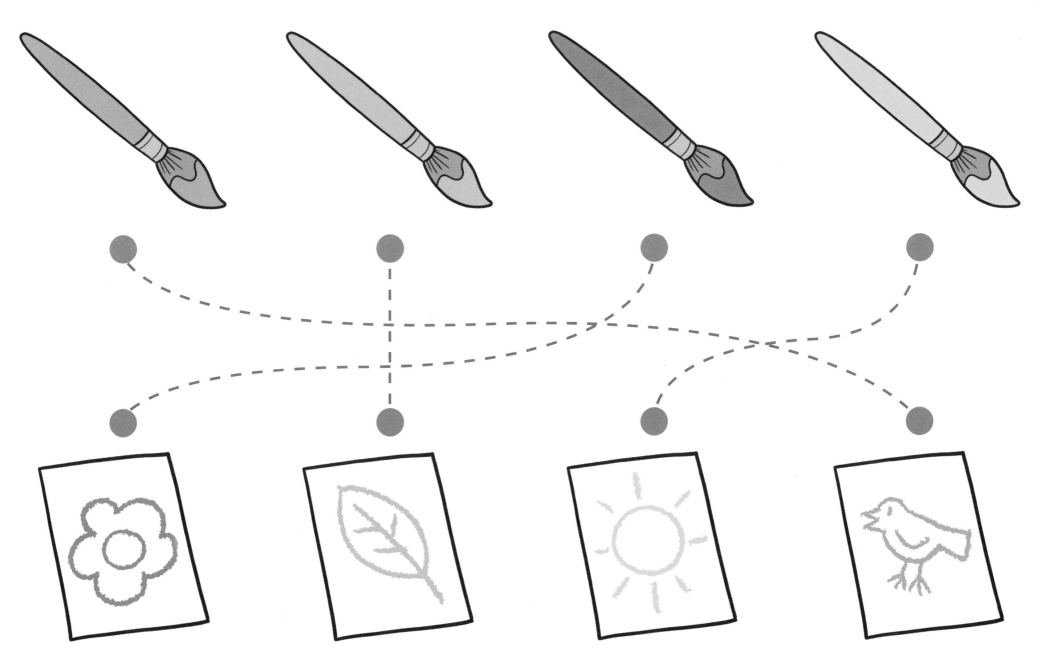

Trace. **Listen.** **Color.**

Look. Circle.

Point. Color. Say.

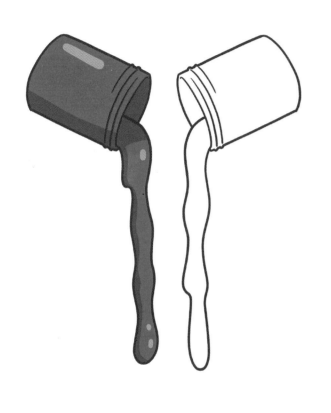

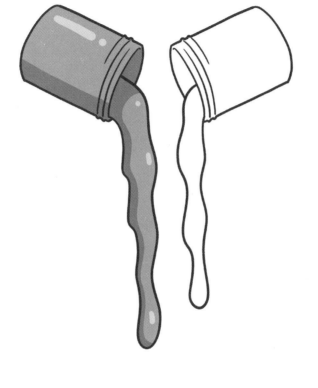

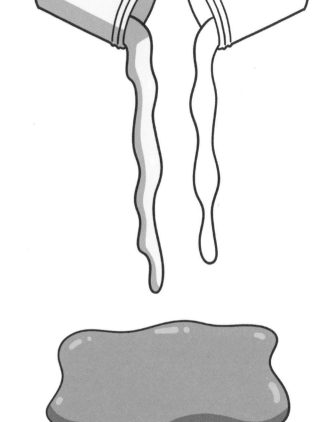

Make. **Say.**

Look.  Color.

Unit 1 Well-being: I feel like there is a lot to look forward to.

2 Our Classroom

 Say. Listen. Color.

Trace. Color. Say.

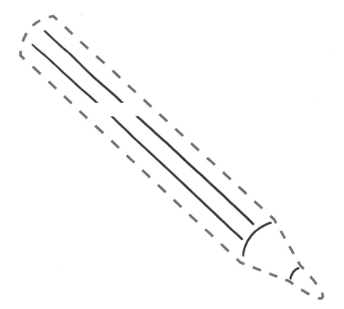

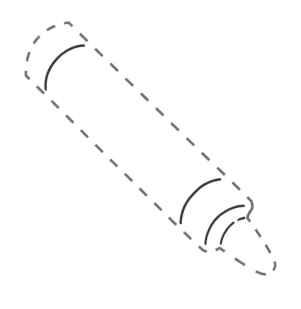

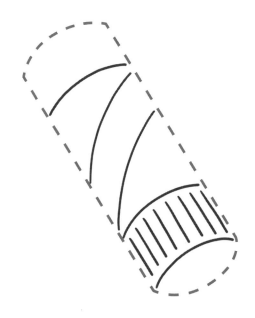

Color. Draw.  Say.

Find. Circle.

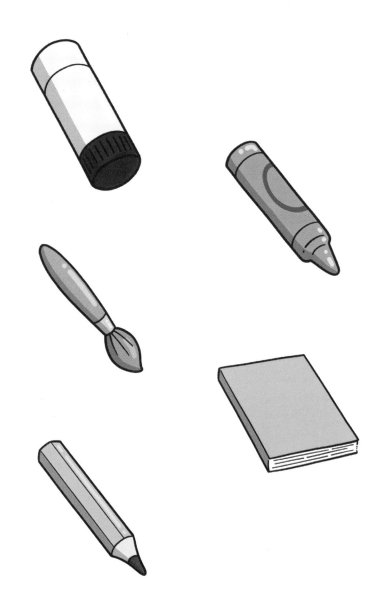

Look. Color.

Say. Trace.  Color.

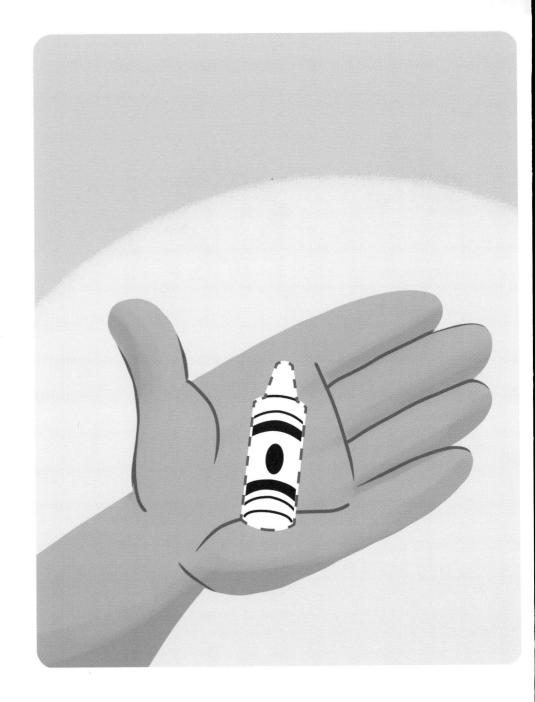

Make.  Say.

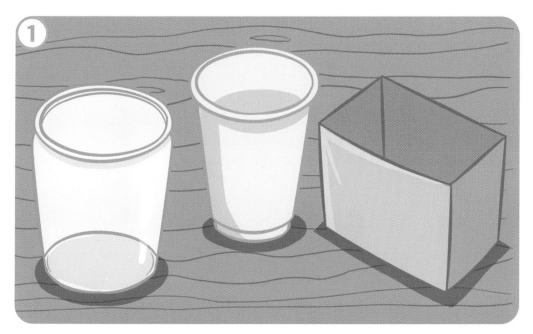

 Draw.

Unit 2 Well-being: I feel like people are friendly.

3 Our Feelings

 Listen. Point. Circle.

Color. Say.

Listen. Trace. Say.

Look. Say.  Match.

Look. Color.

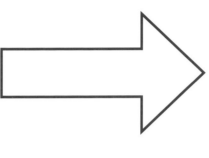

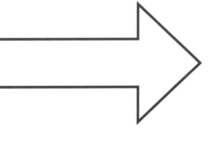

 Listen. Circle. Say.

Make.  Say.

Remember! Color.

4 Our Families

 Say. Listen. Trace.

Listen. Circle. Match.

Draw. Say.

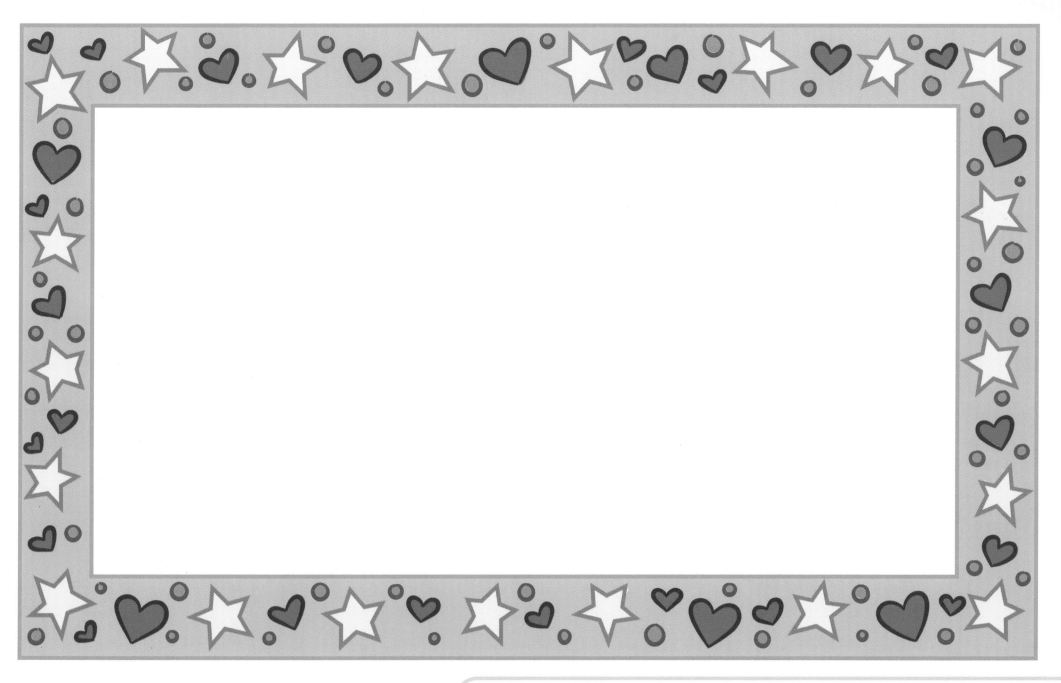

Look.  Match.

Look.  **Circle.**

Look.  Trace.

Make.  **Say.**

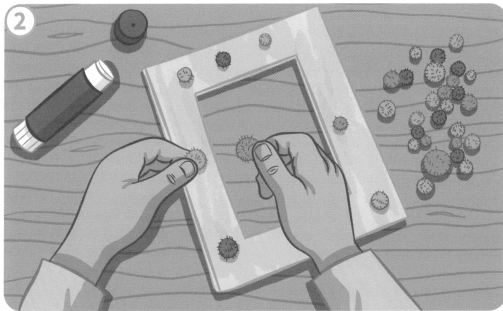

 Look.  Circle.

5 Our Bodies

 Listen. Match. Say.

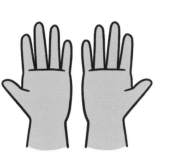   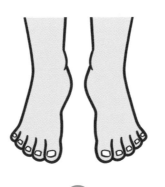  

Count. **Circle.** **Listen.**

 1 2

 3 4

 3 4

Listen. Trace. Color.

Listen. **Point.** **Match.**

 Circle.

Choose. **Circle.** **Listen.**

Unit 5 **Cross-curricular:** physical education

Make.  Say.

Draw. Color.

Unit 5 Well-being: I feel healthy.

6 Our Clothes

 Listen. Point. Color.

Color. Say. Circle.

Listen. **Circle.** **Say.**

Listen. Color. Circle.

Circle.  Mime.

Match.  Say.

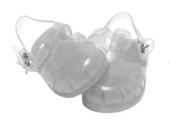     

Make.  Say.

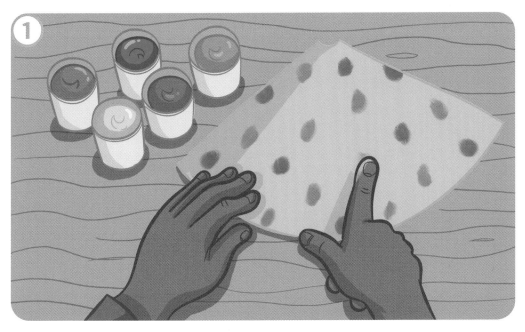

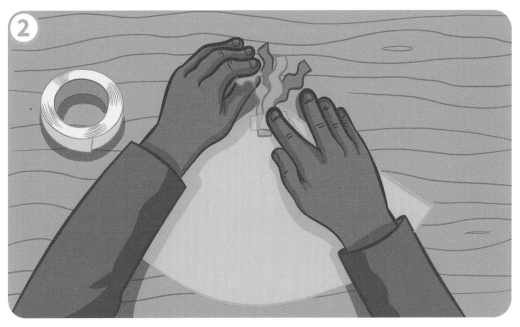

Draw. **Color.**

7 Our Pets

 Count. Circle. Listen.

Trace. Say.

Listen. **Color.** **Circle.**

Listen. **Match.**

Look.  Trace.

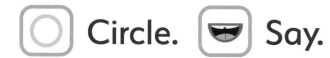 Circle. Say.

Make.  Say.

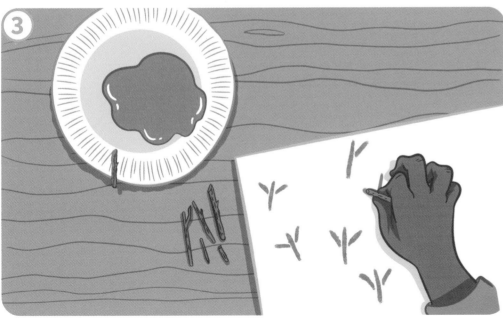

Draw. Color.

8 Our Lunch

 Listen. Circle. Say.

Draw lines. Say.

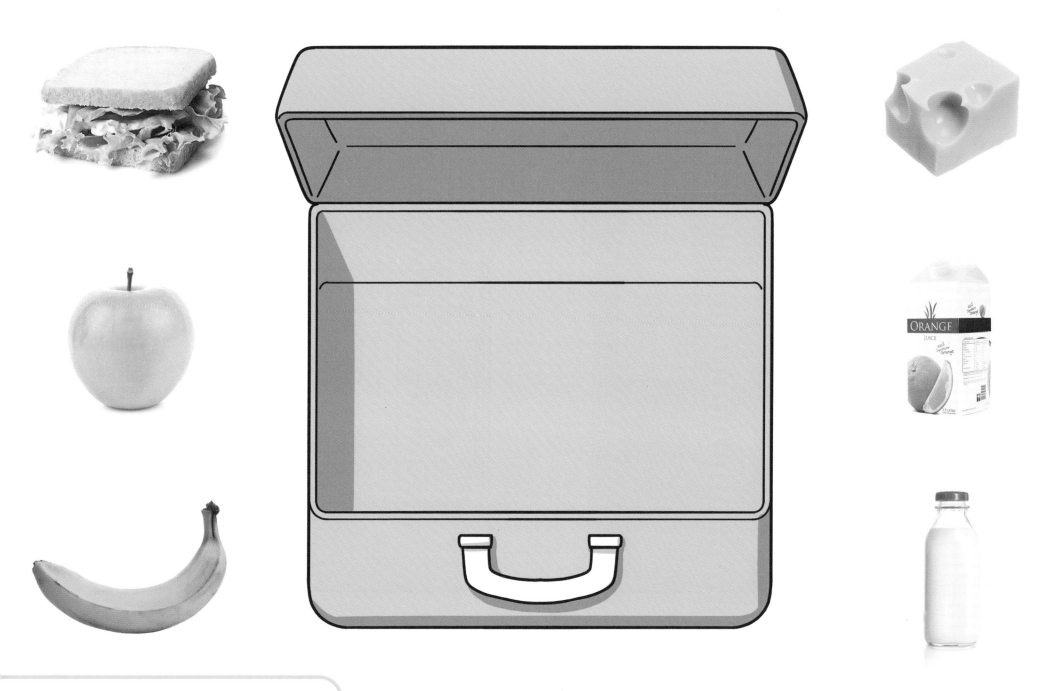

Listen. Say. Trace.

     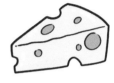

Look. Draw lines. Say.

 Circle. Say.

Make.  Say.

①

②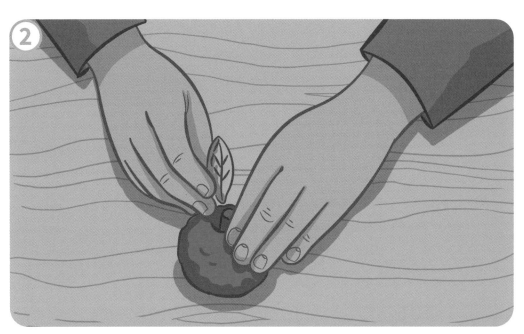

③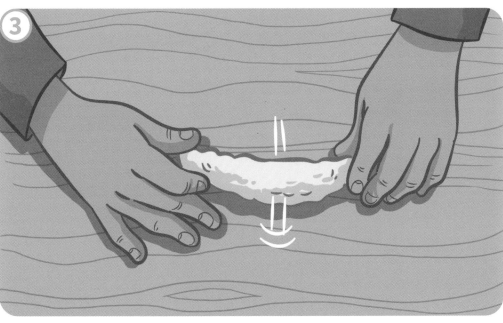

④

Trace. **Draw.** **Color.**

Unit 8 **Well-being:** I feel like I have a lot of energy.

9 Our Toys

 Color. Listen. Say.

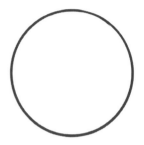

Count. Circle. Say.

Match. Listen. Say.

Language Presentation: What's that? It's a (ball). **Unit 9** 73

Listen. Draw.  Color.

Say. Trace. Match.

Trace. **Color.** **Draw.**

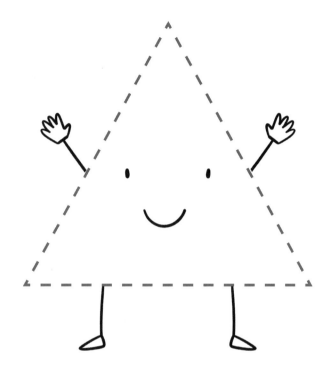

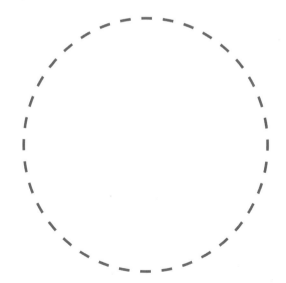

Make.  Say.

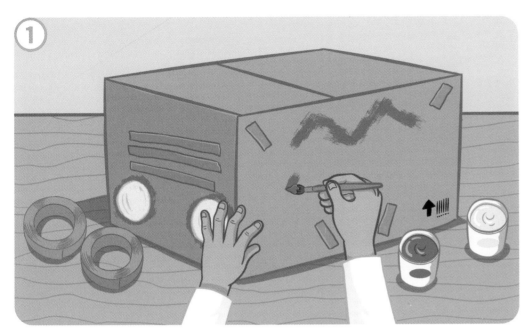

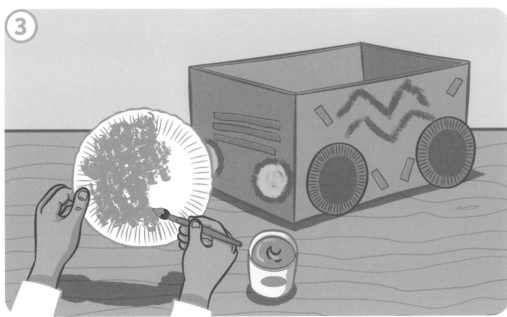

Choose. Trace.

Listen. **Trace.**  **Color.**

G g

Color. Listen. Circle.

Listen. **Trace.** **Color.**

Aa

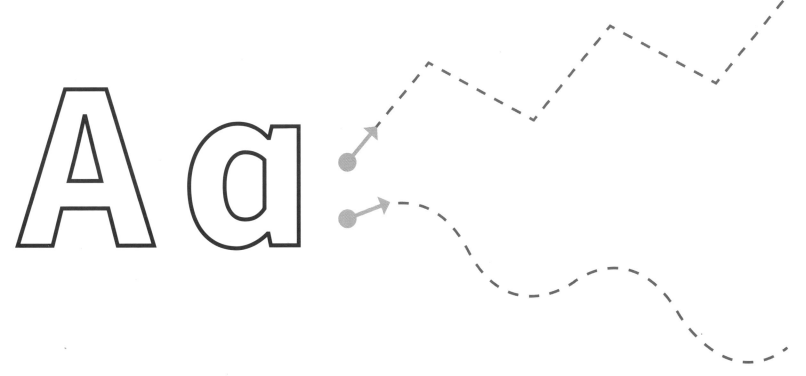

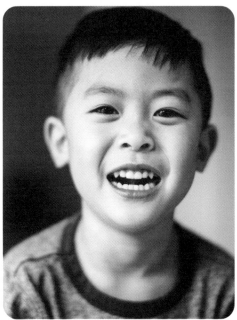

Listen. **Say.**  **Color.**

Listen. **Trace.** **Color.**

Listen. **Trace.** **Color.**

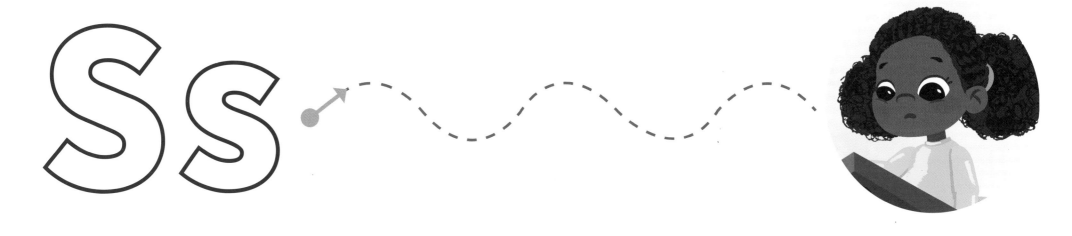

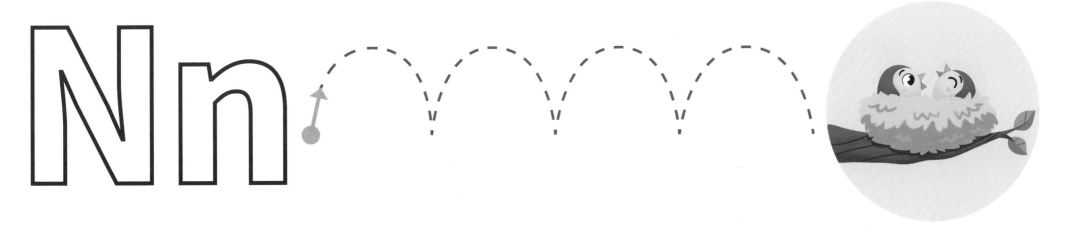

Listen. **Follow.** **Color.**

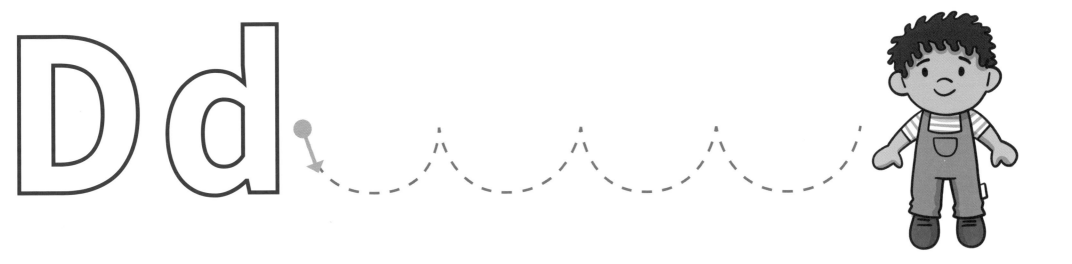

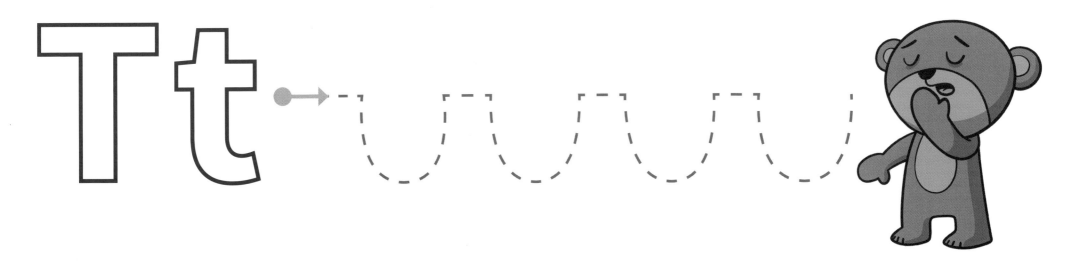

Look. **Color.** **Count.**

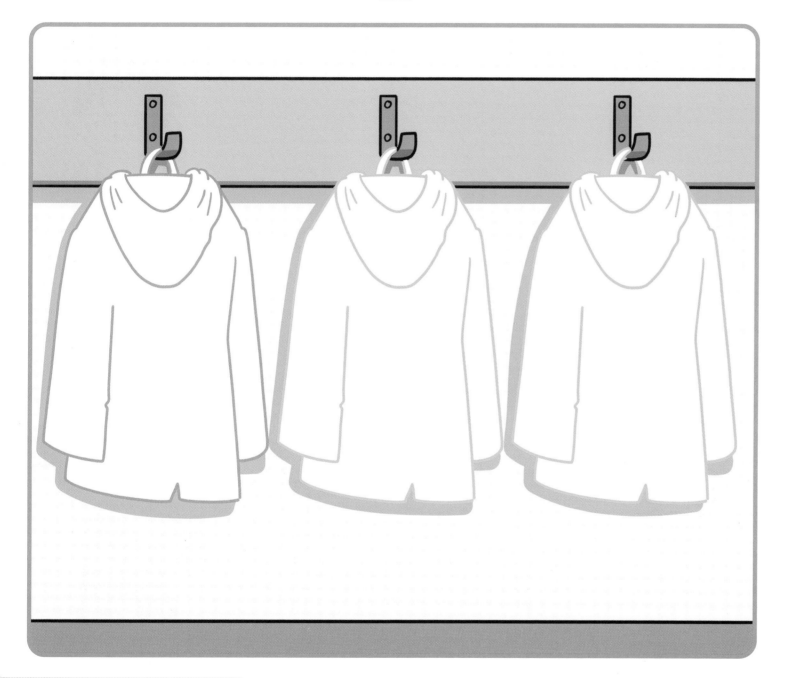

Count. Match. Color.

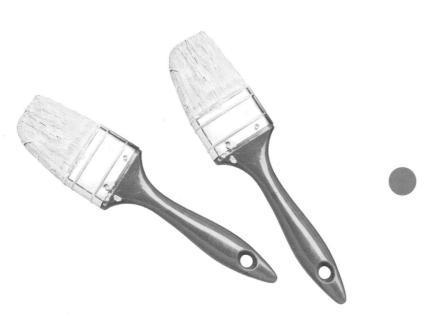

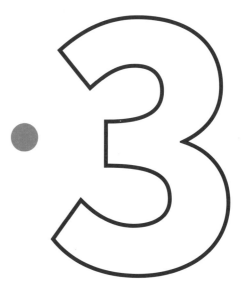

Count. Color.

3

4

Count. Match. Color.

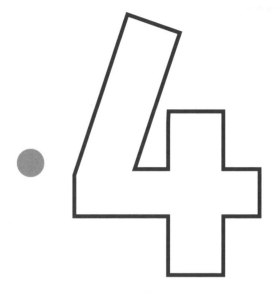

Color. Count. ◯ Circle.

4

5

6

Circle. Count.  Color.

Count. **Match.**  **Color.**

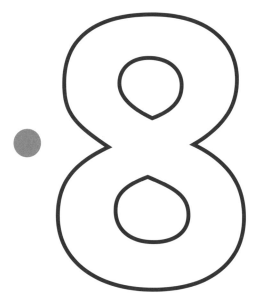

Count. Say. Color.

Count.  Match. Color.

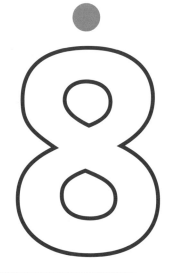  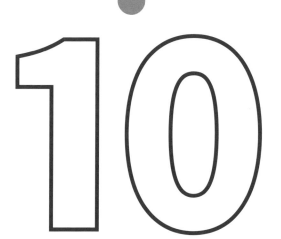